Picture This!

ARCTURUS

This edition published in 2023 by Arcturus Publishing Limited
26/27 Bickels Yard, 151–153 Bermondsey Street,
London SE1 3HA

Author: William Potter
Illustrator: Gareth Conway
Editor: Violet Peto
Designer: Stefan Holliland
Managing Editor: Joe Harris

ISBN: 978-1-3988-1530-8
CH010114NT
Supplier 29, Date 0123, PI 00002160

Printed in China

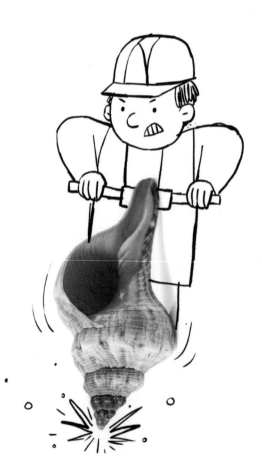

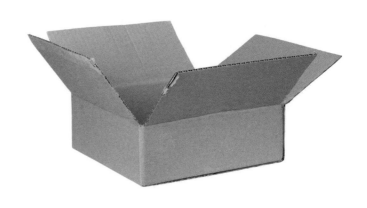

Unleash your imagination by transforming everyday objects into unexpected animals, funny machines, monsters, robots, space rockets, and more!

Get Chopping!

You won't get told off for playing with your food here. What tasty inventions will you come up with?

What would the best-dressed woodland fairy wear?

Why not clown
about with a
tomato as a nose?

Metal Mischief

Get into gear with these nuts, bolts, and cogs, and conjure up some masterworks.

Could a cog become a
face with eyes, cheeks,
and a slurpy tongue?

Fruit Fantasy

What sweet delights could you cook
up with this basket full of fruit?

Could this cherry
become a pooch with
a stalk tail?

Try another banana
boat of your own.

Leafy Look-alikes

Let your imagination go wild with this litter of leaves.

Give me a kiss! This bright red leaf makes a perky pair of lips.

Turn a leaf into
a fuzzy beard.

Juice on the Loose

What juicy ideas will these funky fruits inspire?

If this sunny slice of lemon is too hot, you can always make lemonade!

Time to take off in a tangerine helicopter.

Red sky at night ... a blood orange slice can become a setting sun.

Shell Show

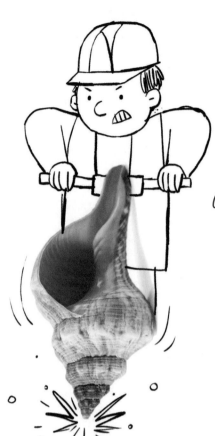

Give these seashells a
new splash of life.

Fill a shell cone
with a scoop of
ice cream.

Is this a shell or a
sneaky octopus in
disguise?

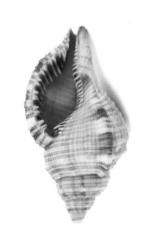

Cookies Galore!

Take a bite, and be creative with these cookies.

Shhh! Don't wake the baby, all snug in her baked bedsheets.

A pair of round cookies makes a great set of wheels.

Bottle Tops

An empty bottle can take on a new life and even take off!

This bottle is ready for blast off: 3-2-1 ...

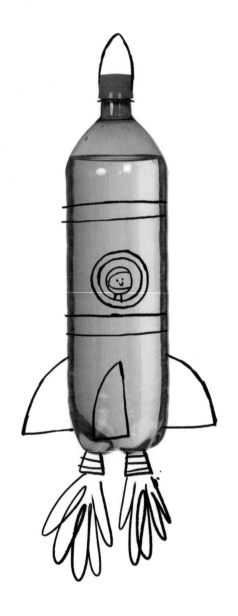

Up periscope!
A bottle on its side
can deep dive as
a submarine.

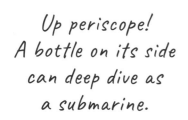

Creative Cones

These pine cones have plenty of potential.

Watch out! Don't step on this rattlesnake!

This boy needs a comb, not a cone!

Wrapper's Delight

Foil-covered candies or bows?
You decide!

Where could
this well-dressed
dressed boy be
off to?

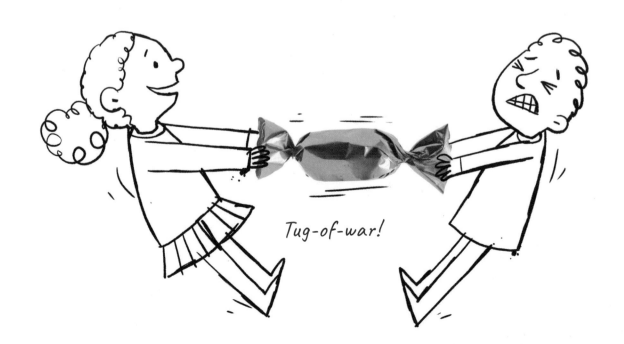

Tug-of-war!

Kooky Kitchen

No recipe required. Add whatever
you like to these kitchen tools.

A whisk could become
a microphone.

Add a few strings,
and this colander
plays like a banjo.

Fungi Fun

Mushrooms make otherworldly ears for an alien.

Time for a spot of tea with your toadstool table.

Upside down, this
fungus becomes a
funky skilift.

Clever with Cakes

Turn these fancy cakes into new creations before they're gobbled up.

How noble this queen looks in her chocolate crown.

A slice provides
a ramp for
a skilled
skateboarder.

Total Nuttiness

Go nuts with cashews, almonds, and walnuts.

A wrinkly walnut resembles a brain.

Could this cashew be
a dinosaur claw?

Silly Socks

Pull your socks up, and come up with a stocking full of arty ideas.

Striped socks or fancy antlers?

This zebra will keep extra warm in its matching wool leggings.

Heads Up

Put your thinking cap on, and come up with some clever hat doodles.

Out of this world!
A hat becomes a UFO.

What washed up on the beach—a hat or a sand castle?

Beat This!

Get into the rhythm, and pencil around percussion.

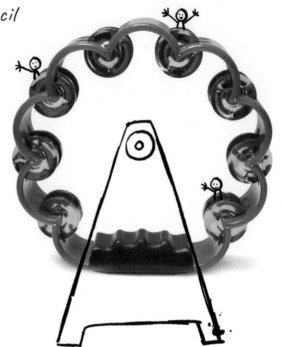

Could this tambourine be a flying saucer?

Turn these bongos
into a bouncy
trampoline!

Made-up Makeup

Can you make makeup as pretty as a picture?

Turn this brush into a lamp with a fringed shade.

38

Could this
eyeshadow
box be a
skyscraper?

School Supplies

Your homework today is to turn school supplies into surprising new things.

Make a splash turning a staple remover into a jet ski.

Could a clip double as
a trendy handbag?

Nothing Goes to Waste

Recycle this waste into new creations.

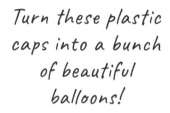

Turn these plastic caps into a bunch of beautiful balloons!

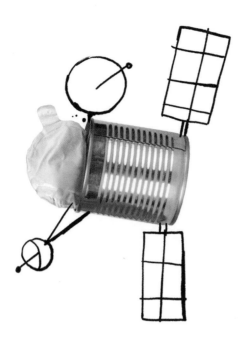

Turn a junk
sardine can into
a junk boat!

Scrub-a-Dub-Dub

Clean up your act by freshening up these products.

Cock-a-doodle-do! This doodle will do.

This plunger is just what Pirate Pete needed!

Arty Actions

Will these paint sets provide artistic inspiration?

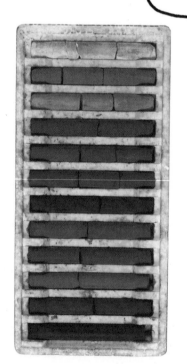

A tube of paint provides a tie for a chic event.

Draw a pianist for this chalk-tray piano.

Cycle Recycle

Can you recycle these bike parts?

Brakes levers or high-heeled shoes?

Get a grip on these handlebars, and turn them into horns.

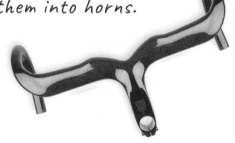

Knock! Knock!

Open your mind, and doodle
over door handles.

Anyone in?
A door knocker
becomes
a striking
earring.

Make this door
knocker into facial
hair, and give it a
face to adorn.

Bright Ideas

Bet you come up with some awesome ways with light bulbs.

A ballerina lights up the stage with her tutu.

Launch this light into space as part of an astronaut's spacesuit.

Pipe Pictures

Ever played
with plumbing?

A pipe with valves
can rocket away
as the base of a
spaceship.

Plumb this pipe into a trumpet frame for a toot or two.

Five short pipes form a crest on a lizard.

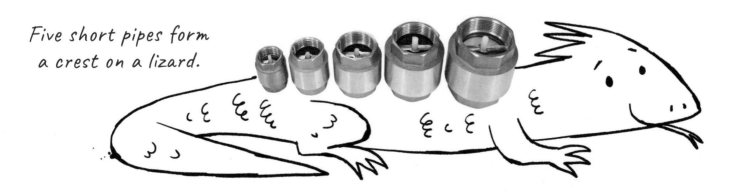

Construction Site

What will you build with the right toolkit?

With blades attached, this drill can power a hovercraft.

The handles
on this tool
make a beak
for a gull.

Key Changes

Unlock the secrets of these classy keys.

Could a large key cause a bus driver to stop?

The king shows off
his ceremonial staff.

Transformed Tech

Give this computer
kit an arty upgrade.

Would a laptop tent be waterproof?

Could this be the camera on a Mars rover?

Like Clockwork

Take time to reinvent these clock parts.

This cog
looks like
the wheel on
an ancient
chariot.

Live Wires

Assemble robots
with switches
and circuits.

A circuit board
could power an
android.

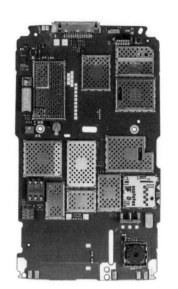

56 KΩ

Eggs-traordinary!

Whisk up some clever ideas adapting eggs.

What weird magic is being brewed by this wacky witch?

Add fins and
watch this egg
swim away.

Light Switch

Don't hang around! These lampshades need a makeover.

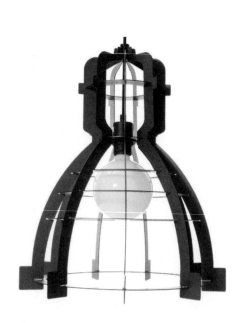

Flip this lampshade for a wonderful wok.

For all your hard work, you deserve an award.

On the Trail

How far will you go with this hiking equipment?

Fill a water bottle with air for a super scuba diver.

You can't beat
a backpack as a
punchbag.

Step up and turn
walking sticks
into stilts.

Garden Grows

What could these garden tools sprout into?

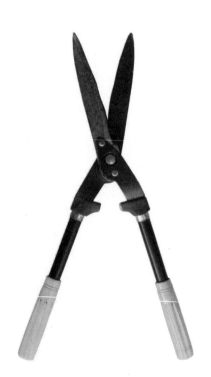

72

Turn a watering can into a crane for some heavy lifting.

Rock out with a trowel guitar.

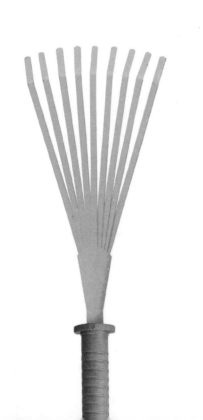

Fast (Food) on the Draw!

What fast-food features
could you cook up?

Try turning these
snacks into wild hair.

Pizza delivery!
Catch it while
it's spinning.

Journey back
to the Jurassic
Period for a tasty
hotdogosaurus.

Rock and Roll

It's a hard choice—what could these rocks become?

Top of the world! Plant your flag on this peak.

What masterpiece will this skilled sculptor shape?

Nice as Ice

What cool, crafty ideas will you have with frozen treats?

Blast off in a roaring rocket.

Could an ice
cream become
a tourist
attraction?

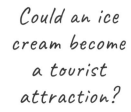

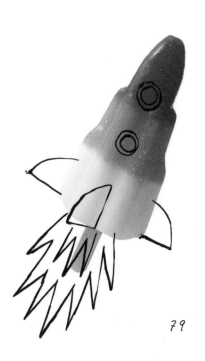

Thirsty Work

Mix up these cocktail decorations.

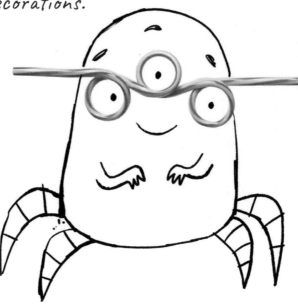

Turn this cocktail stick into a noble knight's sword.

A looped straw could make
spectacular eyewear.

Round and Around

These donuts are more than a sweet treat.

Take your donuts for a spin
as the wheels of a car.

Snack Attack

Take a bite out of
these naughty nibbles.

Saddle up
with a curvy
snack.

Take control of a
pretzel game player.

Playtime

These children's toys could have come from another world ...

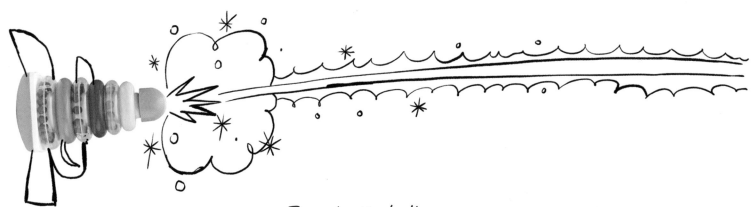

Two plastic balls could become googly eyes for a friendly Martian.

Spice Mix

Here are more ingredients for your masterpieces.

This peppery sheep is sure to sneeze.

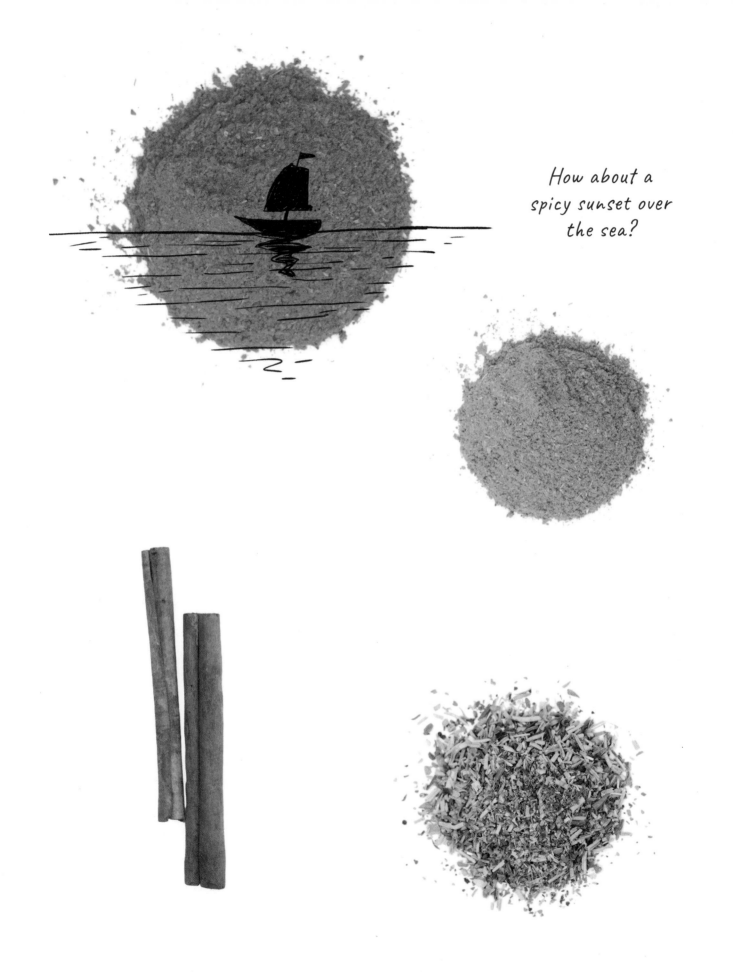

How about a
spicy sunset over
the sea?

Arty Autos

Bolt together these car parts
for some mechanical magic.

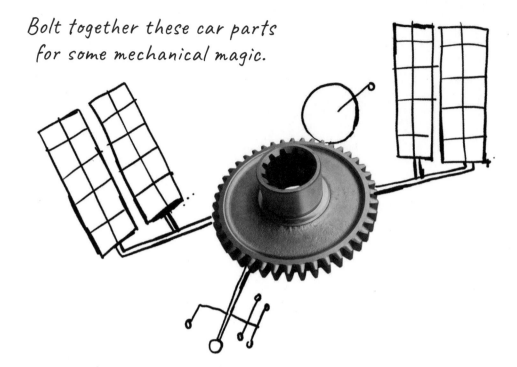

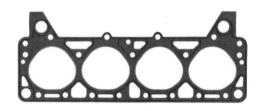

Cast a spell with a
wizard's wand.

Turn pistons into a
creepy-crawly.

Jolly Jewels

Add extra glitter
to gold and gems.

A pair of
earrings or a
ballerina's legs?

Who's looking pretty?

Grape Escape

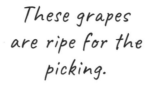

These grapes are ripe for the picking.

Could they be balloons, balls, or wheels?

Stylish Shapes

What arty inspiration can you find in these objects?